Why a Book of Jewish World Records?

The Book of Jewish World Records was created
out of whole cloth to serve two important pur-
poses: (1) to bring to the world a collection of
events and achievements little known, perhaps, but
every bit as important (if not as verifiable) as those
in the splendid *Guinness Book of World Records,*
and (2) to do so with tongue in cheek and a dash
of humor. The Jewish people have always had a
unique talent for laughing at themselves. Their humor, however, is not circumscribed by race or re-
ligion, time or place. Laughter is universal, and as
Ella Wheeler Wilcox wrote way back in 1883

> Laugh and the world laughs with you;
>   Weep, and you weep alone;
> For the sad old earth must borrow its mirth,
>   But has trouble enough of its own.

And *she* wasn't even Jewish!

THE BOOK OF

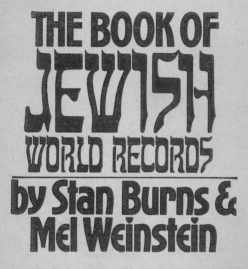

JEWISH

WORLD RECORDS

by Stan Burns & Mel Weinstein

(Members of Writers' Guilt of America)

The one and only book that answers all your questions about the Jewish World and the spectacular accomplishments of the "Chosen People."

A Pinnacle Books/Melvin Powers Publication

PINNACLE BOOKS • LOS ANGELES

THE BOOK OF JEWISH WORLD RECORDS

Copyright © 1978 by Stan Burns and Mel Weinstein

A Pinnacle Books/Melvin Powers Publication edition, published for the first time anywhere.

First Printing, July 1978

ISBN: 0-523-40264-3

Cover illustration by John Dearstyne

Printed in the United States of America

PINNACLE BOOKS, INC.
2029 Century Park East
Los Angeles, California 90067

To our beloved wives, Shirley and Roz, who during the writing of this book, between them established a new world's record for repeating 12,852 times, "From *this* you're gonna make a *living*?"

FOREWORD

The authors' primary purpose in offering *The Book of Jewish World Records* to the public is to settle all those arguments that have caused Jewish people the world over to become exasperated, raise their blood pressure, and develop countless cases of heartburn.

Covering every conceivable subject from A.K. to *zhlub,* this volume will, for the first time, reveal the long-awaited answers to Jewish questions that nobody ever even asked.

IS IT A RECORD?

The records in this book are the result of intensive and exhaustive research by the authors into the realm of pure fantasy. To any person, living, dead, or otherwise, who cares to question the authenticity of the records in this book, all we can say is, if it isn't a record, it's close enough.

TABLE OF CONTENTS

CHAPTER 1
The Human Person

Size

TALLEST GIANTS

Claims concerning the height of Jewish giants are not always founded on accurate information, especially claims about the dead ones. For example, Biblical references seem to indicate that the height of Goliath was either underestimated by early Hebrew chroniclers, or else he lost at least six inches in the translation. It's academic anyway, because Goliath wasn't even Jewish. Other reports by Jewish

3

historians and scholars are likewise unreliable, chiefly because of poetic license and illegible handwriting.

Based on Biblical accounts, the tallest Jew who ever lived was Avram Ben Azuza, whose height, at 16 feet, 4 inches, went unnoticed until he was caught trying to sneak aboard Noah's Ark, paired with a female giraffe.

* * *

SHORTEST GIANT

In 1593, Don Felipe Horowitz, a Sephardic (Spanish Jew) toreador from Madrid, attained the height of 13 feet, 2 inches, encouraged by a Spanish Inquisition interrogation team that leant assistance by helping to stretch him on a torture rack. After confessing to heresy, Don Felipe Horowitz was released from the rack and immediately snapped back to his original height of 5 feet, 9 inches.

* * *

TALLEST GIANTESSES

During a 1972 Holy Land dig, a 7-foot, 7-inch female skeleton was uncovered by archeologist Dr. Leon Sussman. Evidence seemed to lend support to the Biblical *boobe-myseh* (old wives' tale) that this, indeed, was the remains of Rebecca, the woman over whom David slew Goliath because she refused to stop dating a Philistine *shaygets* (Gentile). Before hard proof was forthcoming, however, the completely reassembled skeleton vanished. There was some speculation that Dr. Sussman's wife, Sophie, a simple woman, had inadvertently used the bones to make soup.

* * *

SHORTEST DWARF, MALE

Morris Farbstein, a 42-year-old *apikoros* (skeptic, nonbeliever) of Perth Amboy, New Jersey, is only 22 inches tall. At one time Farbstein was over 6 feet tall, but on March 4, 1967, while on a safari in Africa, this nonbeliever recklessly called a native witch doctor a schmuck.

Weight

MOST WEIGHT GAIN, GROUP

During a one-week period, October 7–14, 1971, aboard the *S.S. Gribenes*, flagship of the Jewish American Princess Lines, a total of 8,250 pounds was gained by 400 couples on a cruise sponsored by the Weight Watchers chapter of a Beverly Hills synagogue.

* * *

HEAVIEST NOSE

The world's heaviest nose belongs to Sidney Katz, age 53, of Brooklyn, New York. For the past 10 years, Mr. Katz has been living in an apartment right over a Jewish bakery in the

Brownsville section of Brooklyn. The savory smells of the freshly baked rye bread, pumpernickel, *challeh,* bagels, rolls, marble cake, Danish, *hamantashen* (prune cakes), etc., inhaled by Mr. Katz had an accumulated count, over a ten year period, of more than 4 billion calories, causing his nose to gain more than 70 pounds. Mr. Katz's nose is the only one in medical history to be operated on for a hernia.

Beginnings

EARLIEST TRANSVESTITE

The first item on the agenda of the Jewish Theological Symposium, held in Nashville on July 18, 1977, was "Genesis—Garden of Eden Revisited." Several revolutionary theories were advanced, among them the thesis that Adam was the first transvestite because two days after he ate the apple he started to wear Eve's fig leaf.

* * *

FIRST PREHISTORIC HEADACHE

The sexual customs of the early *cavemench* (*Homo saperstein*) have been determined from 2-million-year-old hieroglyphs found in a cave in Mesopotamia. Freely translated, the pictures tell the story of how a prehistoric Jewish groom kidnapped and *schlepped* (dragged) his intended bride by the hair to the honeymoon cave. His first passionate wedding night advances involved clubbing her on and about the head into total submission, which caused the bride to *krechtz* (moan) the immortal phrase, "Not tonight, dollink, I've got such a headache."

* * *

EARLIEST JEW

According to the best historical data available, the earliest Jew was Mel Brooks.

* * *

EARLIEST EXPLORERS

Anthropologists have confirmed that one of the Ten Lost Tribes of Israel landed in America at least 2500 years before Columbus. There is mounting evidence that the tribe landed on what is now Miami Beach, where it was met by a tribe of friendly Seminole Indians. Over a period of a few years, the Seminole tribal culture was strongly influenced by Jewish tribal culture. The similarity between the hora, for example, and the Indian rain dance is unmistakable. One unsupported legend has it that the Indians performed a hora/rain dance during a long, dry spell, after which the heavens opened up, and it rained seltzer for 22 days. The lost tribe of Israeli explorers lingered only a short time and then moved on and got lost somewhere else.

Age

OLDEST MAN

At 113 years old, Mendel Puzzis, a resident of the Sol City Retirement Village in Palm Springs, California, is the oldest living Jew on record. Puzzis has his own teeth, his own hair, and has never worn eyeglasses. A health-food faddist, Puzzis attributes his longevity to a limited diet. He eats once a day, and his meal consists of organic *kishka* (tripe) and a dry martini with a prune in it.

*   *   *

OLDEST WOMAN

The oldest woman on record is Mrs. Gertie Friedkin of Long Beach, Long Island, who won't reveal her age because of vanity. However, according to her husband, Max (age 109), Gertie is 113 years old. Max, who refers to his wife as the *alta* (the old one), attributes her age to the fact that she is determined to outlive him for spite, so he shouldn't leave everything to his second wife.

Biblically speaking, Methuselah, at 900 years of age, was supposed to have lived the longest life ever. In more recent history there are many unsubstantiated claims of longevity, the most famous of which is that of the reported 257-year-old Jewish Sherpa of Nepal—Chaim Soham Gurpu—an Orthodox mountain climber. As the story goes, Gurpu was born in the year A.D. 1600, and just prior to his death in 1857, he attributed his longevity to the fact that right up to that very time, he was still alive.

Sex

YOUNGEST SEXUAL ENCOUNTER

The youngest sexual encounter of record is found to take place among Jewish baby boys, usually eight days after birth. It is known as circumcision.

Birth and Parentage

OCTUPLETS

A set of octuplets was born to Mrs. Zelda Tebbish on March 7, 1958, in Cleveland, Ohio (aggregate weight 15 pounds, 6 ounces, with an average of 3 pounds, 11 ounces). There were five girls and one doctor, one lawyer, and one accountant.

TWINS, JEWISH SIAMESE

The only Jewish Siamese twins in the world are Abe and Max Karamazoff, born in 1938 in the Russian Ukraine, joined at the hips. Overcoming this handicap, the brothers undertook religious training, and today, in Louisville, Kentucky, are in great demand in the Jewish religious community as the Siamese Twin Cantors.

*　　*　　*

MOST ADOPTIONS

After 15 years of childless marriage, Mr. and Mrs. Irving Eisenberg of Seattle, Washington, feeling that their lives were empty, adopted 11 children in two years just to fulfill their need for aggravation.

*　　*　　*

OLDEST MAMA'S BOY

The oldest mama's boy is Leon Skeletsky, who lives with his mother, Sadie, in St. Petersburg, Florida. Leon is 52 years old, and he won't be 53 until his mother tells him.

GREATEST *NACHES* (PRIDEFUL PLEASURE)

On October 11, 1972, Mrs. Ida Margolis of Glen Cove, Long Island, returned from shopping with a neighbor, Mrs. Schwartz, to discover that her five-year-old son, Nathan, was playing doctor. Nathan was conducting a complete physical examination on Mrs. Schwartz's nude three-year-old daughter, Naomi. Hurriedly, Mrs. Margolis summoned Naomi's mother to the bedroom and with great pride exclaimed, "Look! My son, the doctor." The following day Mrs. Schwartz filed a malpractice suit against Nathan on behalf of her daughter.

Physical Conditions

LONGEST HEART STOPPAGE

The longest heart stoppage on record was that of Mrs. Sylvia Goldblatt. Mrs. Goldblatt's heart stopped for 3 hours and 17 minutes on April 3, 1957, when she learned she wasn't invited to her daughter's wedding. The intended bride, upon hearing of her mother's complete recovery, suffered a heart attack in turn, and had to postpone the wedding.

RAREST DISEASE

On January 12, 1974, Mrs. Edith Dubinsky was admitted to the Los Angeles Cedars-Sinai Medical Center with a perplexing array of symptoms so complex that the entire medical staff was unable to arrive at a diagnosis. Exhaustive laboratory tests and diagnostic procedures served only to further confuse the medical staff. Five reputable specialists were brought in to evaluate this rare disease, and after six hours of intensive consultation, the specialists finally agreed that Mrs. Dubinsky's unique symptoms were so baffling, they couldn't even decide on a fee.

*   *   *

MOST FAINTING SPELLS

Mendel Kleppenberger, age 33, of Norfolk, Virginia, has fainted more than 6000 times in the past 20 years—an average of six times per week. The fainting spells started at age 13, following Kleppenberger's Bar Mitzvah, when he seriously assumed the religious responsibilities of manhood. An extremely pious man, Kleppenberger so joyously anticipates his morning prayers that he invariably dons his *t'fillin* (phylacteries) in great haste, coiling the leather straps much too tightly around his left forearm, thereby cutting off the blood supply to his brain.

WORST HYPOCHONDRIAC

Among hypochondriacs, Morris Mandlebaum has compiled a record unrivaled in modern times. Beginning as six-time poster boy for the Mount Sinai Foundation for Jewish Complaints, Mandlebaum reached his peak in 1974, when he consumed 27,236 pills, drank 8,327 bottles of medicine, and paid 732 visits to various doctors and specialists. He also carried in his pocket a total of 672 current wallet-size X-rays. Mr. Mandlebaum's record-breaking hypochondria is all the more remarkable considering the fact that he enjoyed poor health right up to the time he died from natural symptoms in 1977 at the ripe old age of 105.

AFFLICTIONS

Most dreaded Jewish disease is the swine flu.

* * *

Most dreaded *yenta's** disease is lockjaw.

* Yenta: Gossip monger; busybody; non-stop talker.

Most dreaded affliction for a Jewish husband is his wife's total recall.

* * *

Most dreaded plastic surgery is performed by husbands cutting up their wives' credit cards.

* * *

Most dreaded sound to a Jewish mother is her daughter's new boyfriend's name: Guiseppe.

* * *

Most dreaded hereditary condition is a psychosomatic disorder found chiefly among Jewish children: terminal guilt.

TEETH

LARGEST FALSE

The largest false teeth in existence are the dental plates belonging to Bronxite Lester Leventhal, who at night soaks his dentures in a 5-gallon seltzer bottle.

The most sets of false teeth are owned by Abe Gutterman, a 77-year-old Orthodox Jew. Mr. Gutterman has seven separate sets of dentures, each one for a special purpose. These include:

Type	Usage
Milchedik	For dairy foods
Flayshig	For meat
Pareveh	For neutral food
Pesachdik	For Passover food
Chometzdik	For forbidden Passover food
Trayf	For forbidden nonkosher food

Plus one special set of false teeth which Mr. Gutterman uses strictly for fasting on Yom Kippur.

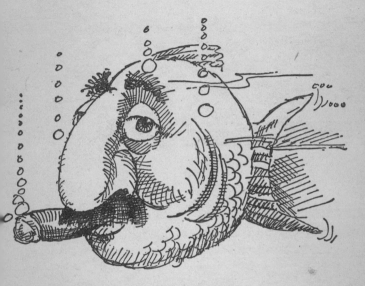

CHAPTER 2
The Animal and Plant Families

Uncommon Animals

RAREST

It is the consensus of zoologists that the rarest animal in the world is a live mink in Miami.

*   *   *

FASTEST

The fastest clocked ground speed for a land animal is 87.5 mph, achieved by a fat, kosher, soup chicken during a common cold epidemic in the Bronx.

LONGEST WEARING

The longest-wearing fur was an albino ranch mink stole, an anniversary gift to Mrs. Sadye Hershkowitz of Collins Avenue, Miami Beach, Florida, from her husband. Given to her on July 8, 1976, she wore it continuously through July 29, during an unprecedented heat wave.

*   *   *

MOST VALUABLE

The highest-priced animal pelt is the crossbred mink-sable (*Neimus Marcus*), whose habitat is chiefly on the fifth floor of a department store in Dallas, Texas.

Household Pets

HEAVIEST JEWISH DOG

The heaviest Jewish dog known was a one-pound, foundling cocker which grew to a weight of 347 pounds in just seven months of feeding on table scraps following its adoption by Nate and Al's Delicatessen in Beverly Hills, California.

* * *

RICHEST DOG

Dr. Harvey Gritzman of Palm Springs, California, who died in March 1969, left his entire estate of $685,000 to his faithful 13-year-old Doberman Pinscher, Farfel. When Farfel died in 1971, the balance of the dog's estate, befittingly, was used to plant trees in Israel.

* * *

MOST ORTHODOX CAT

A seven-year-old Chaimese cat named Yussel, belonging to Mr. and Mrs. Sydney Finkle of San Diego, California, has been raised from kittenhood to observe the strictly kosher dietary laws that prevail in the Finkle household. As a result of this Orthodox upbringing, whenever Yussel pounces on a mouse, he just holds it and patiently waits for the *shochet* (butcher) to arrive and make it kosher.

* * *

DOMESTICATED BIRDS

MOST DEDICATED CHICKEN

The most-dedicated chicken on record is Bertha, a 12-pound, white Leghorn family pet belonging to the Cantor family, who live on an Israeli kibbutz. Just prior to Passover, the devoted Bertha attempted to fill the Cantor family's holiday order for six dozen eggs. In an all-out effort, Bertha laid 105 standard Grade AA extra-large double-yolked eggs in a 24-hour period. She also laid one large heart-shaped egg, which, on closer examination, turned out to be her heart.

* * *

MOST RELIGIOUS

The world's most religious bird is a male parrot named Yankel, age 38. Yankel was raised by his owner, Rabbi Solomon Weisman of Temple Zion in Miami Beach, Florida, and is fluent in both Yiddish and Hebrew. Since Yankel's Bar

Mitzvah, he has proved invaluable to the rabbi and the entire congregation, with his ability to fill in at *minyans* (religious quorums), to deliver sermons in Yiddish, conduct services in Hebrew, and in an emergency even blow the *shofar* (ram's horn) on the High Holidays.

* * *

Most Talkative

The world's most talkative bird is a 97-year-old parrot named Gittle, who resides in the Shalom Retirement Home in Fort Lauderdale, Florida. Gittle, a blue-tinted, open-throated yenta-bird, is a common species (*Groisseh Pisk*, or Big Mouth) in the area, famous for starting arguments, spreading rumors, and preventing conversational lulls.

Pet Owners

MOST CONSIDERATE

Shirley Rosenbaum, a 70-year-old widow in Elmont, Long Island, has overcome her loneliness by enjoying the companionship of her two pet Rhode Island Red chickens, Rosalie and Rebecca. During the 1977 cold spell, one of the chickens caught a bad cold, so Mrs. Rosenbaum killed the other one to make hot chicken soup for the sick one.

Jewish Fish

LARGEST, SEA

The Jewfish, a variety of sea bass, is found in warm seas and has been known to reach gigantic proportions. The largest Jewfish ever caught weighed 872 pounds and was landed by Seymour Blumenfeld on December 15, 1975, off Miami Beach. During the winter months large schools of Jewfish migrate to the Miami area because the warm waters are such a *mechaieh* (great pleasure) for arthritic fins.

*   *   *

LARGEST, FRESH WATER

Since Biblical times there have been innumerable reports of sightings in the Holy Land's River Jordan of the so-called Lox Nosh monster, purportedly measuring up to 22 feet in length and weighing as much as 2 tons. According to Israeli marine biologists, the Lox Nosh monster is believed to be a species of Great White salmon (*Aquus Bagelus*). Legend has it that the Lox Nosh monster is a primitive, nonstop eating machine that gorges itself daily year round, except on Yom Kippur, when it fasts.

Plant Life

PLANTS, FASTEST SPREADING

The fastest-spreading of all plants is the rare
Wandering Jew plant (*Schnell Israelia*), found
in all parts of the globe and dating back 2000
years. The plant grows in all directions at the
rate of 10 feet an hour. On July 12, 1973, a
Wandering Jew plant took root in the Washington, D.C., area where, in 72 hours, the plant
covered more than 68 acres. Strangely, the
Wandering Jew plant abruptly stopped growing
just short of the property line on which the
Egyptian embassy is situated.

*   *   *

TREES, OLDEST

The oldest known living tree is a species of
Joshua tree recently found growing in a remote
corner of the Sinai Desert. Israeli botanist Professor Avrum Fromkin has estimated that the
tree is at least 6200 years old. His finding are
confirmed not only by the tree-ring datings,
but also by an ancient carving of an arrow-
pierced heart, which bears the inscription,
"Adam Loves Eve."

CHAPTER 3

The World of Nature

Natural Wonders

VOLCANOES, HEALTHIEST

The healthiest volcano in the world is the now-extinct Mt. Gezunt, in the Holy Land. Mt. Gezunt acquired its reputation as "healthiest" in 2000 B.C., when it was still an active volcano. Legend has it that a tribe of nomadic Hebrews living at the base of the mountain forsook their vows to one God and reverted to pagan worship, appeasing the fire god on the mountain with daily sacrifices of virgin chickens in the steaming hot crater. Finally, the fire god, *ongeshtupt* (overstuffed) with virgin chickens, erupted, spewing hot chicken soup and molten *schmaltz* (chicken fat) over the entire countryside, providing immunity against illness of any kind to the nomadic Hebrews and all succeeding generations.

INLAND SEAS, SALTIEST, KOSHER

The Dead Sea (394 square miles) is believed by geologists to contain the world's largest kosher salt deposits. This inland "Salt Sea Of the Old Testament" has long intrigued Biblical scholars. The dominant theory now places the Biblical cities of Sodom and Gomorrah under the southern waters of the Dead Sea. The most recently recovered Dead Sea Scroll lends solid support to this theory. Loosely translated from ancient Hebrew, this newest Dead Sea Scroll reads:

> The Fate of Lot's wife was *her* fault.
> She looked back on Sodom—*gevalt*.
> That one glance would kill her
> She turned to a pillar
> Of Sodomy chloride—or salt.

*   *   *

UNDERGROUND SELTZER SPRINGS, MOST PUNCTUAL

In 1908 a natural underground seltzer spring was discovered in the Catskill Mountains in New York. The spring, dubbed the "Alta Kocker," can be depended upon for its punctuality. Every hour on the half-hour, it emits a satisfied *greptz* (belch).

Unorthodox Weather

MOST-DEVASTATING HURRICANE

On November 4, 1973, after the disastrous hurricane season in the Caribbean, the final and most devastating hurricane (and the only one bearing a Jewish name—Zelda) struck Miami Beach with 110-mph winds. After Zelda flattened Miami Beach, the only buildings left standing were two synagogues and a corner candy store.

TEMPERATURE

HOTTEST INDOOR

The hottest indoor temperature was recorded on December 12, 1974, during a card game played by the Hadassah women in the Temple Beth Golem social room in Fargo, North Dakota. A temperature of 197°F. was reached when all of the ladies present experienced hot flashes simultaneously.

*   *   *

COLDEST INDOOR

The coldest indoor temperature on record was —23°F., recorded in the living room of Mr. and Mrs. Ira Levine of Perth Amboy, New Jersey, on February 3, 1968, when their only son, Seymour, introduced them to his new bride, a *shiksa* (gentile girl)!

CHAPTER 4

The Solar System and Space Program

Planets

COLDEST

The coldest planet within our own solar system is Pluto, which has an estimated surface temperature of —360°F. The astronomers at the Israeli Observatory atop Mt. Ramon have advanced the hypothesis that the extreme cold on Pluto is due to the fact that it is inhabited by a lost tribe of Jewish landlords, who refuse to turn on the heat.

Space Travel

COSTLIEST

The projected budget for sending the first Jewish space explorer to galaxies beyond our own *"Milchedik"* (Milky Way) has been tagged at more than $80 trillion by the Israeli Space Agency Independent Accounting Headquarters (ISAIAH). The reason given for the astronomical cost of this venture is that the trip includes meals.

* * *

ROCKETRY AND MISSILES: PROPELLANTS, MOST POWERFUL

The Israeli government is testing a new missile fuel capable of developing incredible energy and force. The formula, while top secret, is known to contain such ingredients as chicken fat, freshly ground horseradish, and 100-proof Slivovitz (cherry brandy). The fuel was recently tested in a projectile, which allegedly attained a velocity faster than the speed of light, until it self-destructed because of heartburn.

CHAPTER 5

Science: Past/Present

Excavations

EARLIEST FEMALE

A female skull was accidentally uncovered during an oil exploration in Beverly Hills, California, on October 7, 1958. Archeologists from UCLA have estimated the age of the skull at more than 22,000 years. Through carbon measuring techniques, they also have ascertained that the skull belonged to a 5-foot, 5-inch girl in her late teens, weighing approximately 140 pounds. Predicated on the discovery of a primitive nose job, wooden orthodontic braces on the teeth, and transparent fish-scale contact lenses, the consensus is that this was the first Jewish American Princess.

EARLIEST CIVILIZATION

The earliest civilization was discovered on October 14, 1976, by a Turkish archeological expedition that set out to confirm sightings of Noah's Ark on Mt. Ararat. At the foot of the mountain, the expedition stumbled across what appeared to be ruins of an ancient civilization. Further investigation of uncovered relics dated the civilization as far back as 8000 B.C. and established beyond any doubt that this was the location of the earliest Jewish civilization. Incontrovertible proof of this fact was the discovery of the skeletal remains of a shopping center and a collection of expired fossilized credit cards.

* * *

OLDEST FURNITURE

The archeological dig at the ancient Biblical site of Jericho revealed (at the fourth level) artifacts of a civilization dating back to 1200 B.C. This was the time of Joshua's conquest of the city of Jericho and its occupation by the Israelites. To archeologists, the most fascinating items uncovered were an upholstered sofa and two upholstered chairs, intact and perfectly preserved, still protected by the original plastic covers.

*   *   *

FIRST JEWISH PIRATE

Early American history records that during the War of 1812, an Orthodox Jew named Morganstern the Pirate plundered Atlantic Coast shipping lanes. He was famed for his black beard and *payess* (Jewish sideburns) and for the large black patch worn over his right eye, which did double duty as a *yarmulke* for morning prayers and holidays. Morganstern, a ruthless buccaneer, supposedly accumulated a huge fortune, which he buried on the beach of what is now Atlantic City, New Jersey. In 1953 a treasure-hunting expedition uncovered a buried chest that is believed to have been part of Morganstern's booty because when opened, it was found to contain more than $50 million in pledges.

Substances

GEMS, GREATEST DISPLAY

On September 4, 1977, at the Sinai Temple's annual Sisterhood dinner-dance, Mrs. Molly Budovsky of Shaker Heights, Ohio, achieved a world record with 92 eye-catching hand positions as she ostentatiously displayed her new 8-carat diamond ring. Among Mrs. Budovsky's innovative manual maneuvers were: the "Calling-the-Waiter-Over" flourish; the "Nonchalant-Back-of-the-Chair" hand-dangle; the "Removal-of-Foreign-Object-from-the-Eye" pretext; the "Brandishing-of-the-Steak-Knife" vulgarity; the "Waving-of-the-Hand-at-Friends" ploy; the "Casual-Yawn-Stifling" flash.

*　　*　　*

MOST ABSORBENT MATERIAL

Exhaustive tests by an independent laboratory show that the most absorbent cloth in the world is a plain linen handkerchief, which has the phenomenal capacity to absorb 10,000 times its own weight in a Jewish mother's tears.

Sounds

LOUDEST *GREPTZ* (BELCH)

On July 16, 1977, clothing salesman Joel
Kravitz ate a full meal at a Hungarian restaurant on Fairfax Avenue in Los Angeles. At the
L.A. airport, Kravitz noshed some kosher junk
food while waiting for his flight to depart.
Aboard the plane, he ate another full meal just
prior to the plane's landing at Kennedy International in New York City. As the overstuffed
Kravitz deplaned, he emitted a supersonic
greptz (SSG) of an intensity that exceeded by
150 decibels the noise of the English/French
Concorde. The *greptz* broke all the windows
within a five-mile radius of the airport. The
New York Port Authority immediately issued
an order forbidding Kravitz from landing at
Kennedy International Airport any time that
he has eaten a meal aboard an incoming plane.

Cameras

FASTEST

In 1971 Professor Yehudah Laskar of Brandeis University, New York, invented a high-speed camera capable of taking 25 million pictures per second. The camera is used in laser, ballistic, and microbiological research. The ultimate test of the speed of this camera was its flawless performance at a Jewish wedding, where it photographed in one-millionth of a second a fully laden table of hors d'oeuvres before it could be stripped clean by a swarm of voracious wedding guests.

Miniaturization

SMALLEST MATZOH

The world's smallest matzoh is a prototype
developed by the Tokyo division of the Manischewitz conglomerate. This miniaturized
matzoh, though no bigger than a microdot, is
fully transistorized, with unleavened printed
circuits and chicken *schmaltz* terminals. Con-
sidered a fantastic technological breakthrough,
this tiny matzoh, although electronically perfect, has, to date, been found to serve no use-
ful purpose.

Computers

LONGEST ODDS

Professor Heinrich Lieberman, who heads the Mathematics Division at M.I.T. (Mavin Institute of Technology), spent three years programming the institution's sophisticated computer with Jewish cultural data. The computer read-out confirmed, among other things, that the odds are 3,750,000,000 to 1 against a Jewish woman being caught dead in the lobby of the Fountainbleu Hotel in Miami Beach, during the height of the tourist season, in a cloth coat.

FASTEST

The fastest computer on record was found to be the brain of Mrs. Bella Livinsky of Riverdale, New York. Mrs. Livinsky, in a single glance at the mountain of gifts presented by guests at her daughter's wedding shower, assimilated, collated, and performed 22 million complex calculations in .003 seconds and arrived at the exact total value of:

15 toasters
17 electric irons
 6 sets of starter service
49 matching towel sets
33 king-sized bedspreads
 8 salad bowls
 6 blenders
14 electric can openers
11 complete sets of Teflon cookware
37 miscellaneous gift certificates.

The total value—$15,756.32—was exactly $311.02 more than her first daughter received.

GREATEST GOSSIP MEMORY BANK

Selma (Yenta-Bird) Tellabendeh of Delancy
Street on the Lower East Side of New York
City has a storehouse of eavesdroppings,
rumors, and gossip second to none. She can
babble from memory 32,456 separate items
about everyone else's business. To avoid repe-
tition Selma keeps an accurate tally by count-
ing every item mentioned on a specially
designed set of Yenta Beads.

Weapons

DEADLIEST

On March 15, 1976, the Israeli military tested a new secret weapon said to be the world's deadliest. The weapon has the capability of completely immobilizing any enemy force. It was developed in Israel at M.I.T. (Mavin Institute of Technology) by psychic physicists. The key to the development of this weapon was found in an intensive study of the emotional reactions of Jewish mothers under stress. The scientists succeeded in isolating the powerful psychic energy waves that emanate from the deadly optical force of a Jewish mother's paralyzing mind-piercing glower when her runaway 16-year-old daughter suddenly appears, eight months pregnant, and introduces the unmarried father, who is a *shaygets* (gentile). Once isolated, this powerful psychic energy was harnessed, converted into a laser beam, and adapted to a hand-held weapon called the JM1 (Jewish Mother 1). When the paralyzing optical psychic energy of the laser beam is targeted on an enemy, it transfixes him and reduces him to a sweating, cowering, weeping, sniveling, guilt-ridden hulk.

CHAPTER 6

Fine Arts
and Show Business

Most Photographs

The largest collection of photographs on record are the 3,427 framed wallet-size pictures of grandchildren, owned by Becky Moses of Syracuse, New York, and carried around by her in a huge shopping bag. Grandma Moses corners total strangers in supermarkets and forces them to look at her pictures.

Portraits

HIGHEST PRICE

The highest price for a painting was paid at an auction that took place at the Eisenstein Galleries in Boston, Mass., on July 5, 1973. Art collector Mrs. Rhoda Lastfogel paid $6,250,-000 for Leonardo Levinsky's original masterpiece entitled *Mona Leah*, because it had two coats of paint.

*   *   *

LONGEST SITTING

Mrs. Esther Bloomgarten, of Atlanta, Georgia, sat for a portrait of herself four hours a day, five days a week for an entire year, or a total of more than 1000 hours. Bruno Berkowitz, the frustrated artist, complaining about the unreasonable length of time taken to finish the portrait, said, "Mrs. Bloomgarten couldn't decide on the colors."

The Spoken Word

MOST COMMON USAGE

The three words most frequently used by Jewish women shoppers are:

- *only*
- *regular*
- *saved*

These three words are normally included in a woman's traditional statement to her husband. For example:

"Look at the suede purse I just bought. It *only* cost $25. The *regular* price is $85. I *saved* $60, and with the $60 I saved, I bought a pair of suede shoes to match."

* * *

FIRST FOOD OFFERING

The first spoken food offering, according to Biblical account, took place in the Garden of Eden, when the serpent said to Adam, "Here, take a piece fruit; you'll enjoy!"

The Written Word

MOST PLAGIARIZED AUTHOR

Recently discovered manuscripts in England reveal the existence of an unheralded sixteenth-century Jewish literary genius named Abraham Glitzman who, if not directly plagiarized, was at least ghostwriter for the most famous literary names of his time. Borrowing shamelessly from Glitzman's works were such contemporaries as Queen Elizabeth, Sir Walter Raleigh, Edmund Spenser, Christopher Marlowe, and even William Shakespeare. As an example, most of the dialogue of Shakespeare's *Taming of the Shrew* was lifted almost verbatim from Glitzman, as illustrated by Glitzman's original line (thinly disguised by the Bard), "That's funny, Katelleh dollink, you don't *look* Shrewish."

Film Industry

LARGEST STUDIO

The largest motion picture lot in the world, located on the outskirts of Tel Aviv, is the Metro-Golda-Meir Studios. The back lot contains 432 buildings, 35 sound stages, and 3 synagogues. The current production will be the most expensive film ever made. The cost will exceed $100 million, and the film will be an outer-space science-fiction extravaganza entitled, *The Star of David Wars.*

Circus

JEWISH CONTORTIONIST

The world's only Jewish contortionist, 57-year-old Ben Herzog, who performed with the famous Israeli Birnbaum and Bialy Circus, suffered a fatal heart attack while attempting a new intertwining stunt for the entertainment of the guests at the wedding of two fellow circus performers. Herzog, after brushing himself with egg yolk and sprinkling himself with poppy seeds, braided himself into a giant-size wedding *challeh* (sabbath bread). The effort of this virtuoso performance proved to be too great a physical strain for Herzog, who suffered a seizure and died in his own arms.

Recordings

FASTEST-SELLING RECORD

The world's record for the fastest-selling recording belongs to Maximillian Schnell of Haifa, who is known in Israel as the "Singing *Mohel*" (circumciser). On April 19, 1977, an original Hebrew folk song recorded by Schnell was released; it sold 3 million copies in two days in Israel alone. The song is called "Maxelleh the *Messer*" (Mack the Knife). Translated into English, the lyric reads:

> Oh, that shark bite
> With those teeth white
> And those big jaws
> What a *fresser**
> But that shark bite
> Cannot cut like
> Good old Maxelleh the *Messer*.

* Eater.

CHAPTER 7

Architectural Overachievements

Buildings

LARGEST HOSPITAL

The largest medical center in the world is the recently completed Denver Jewish Memorial Hospital, costing $230 million and founded by the efforts of the International Jewish Hospital Funding Committee. The hospital complex consists of 13 separate wings, one of which contains 2000 beds; the other 12 wings are devoted entirely to brass plaques honoring donors.

MOST MODERN NURSING HOME

The recently completed Retirement Home
for Aging Yentas, on Beverly Boulevard in
Los Angeles, is believed to offer the most
modern facilities for the comfort of its guests.
The medical equipment was custom designed
and the entire staff expertly trained to cater to
every conceivable need for the elderly *yentas*.
The sophisticated services offered may be best
illustrated in the intensive-care ward, where
three times a day *yentas* are fed rumors in-
travenously.

*   *   *

LARGEST SYNAGOGUE

The recently completed Temple Maccabee in
Westchester County, New York, has over
300,000 square feet of building space for worship and community activities. The entire complex occupies more than 700 acres, and when
all of the facilities are used, upwards of 35,000
people can be accommodated. There is parking
space for 12,500 Cadillacs.

Unique Structures

TALLEST *MEZUZAH**

The tallest *mezuzah* in the world measures 137 feet high by 18 feet wide by 5 feet thick. This huge *mezuzah* is erected on the roof of Miami's newest and largest condominium, the King David Towers, and serves all 350 apartments as a master *mezuzah*.

---

* Miniature replica of the Torah, which contains a copy of the Ten Commandments and is nailed outside the door to ward off evil and non-Jewish suitors of resident daughters.

LONGEST SKI RUN

In the Catskill Mountains in New York state, Grossinger's Resort has just completed the world's largest artificial ski slope, designed to accommodate ardent ski buffs on a year-round basis. The ski slope, a steep, winding run more than two miles long, is maintained with a permanent 16-inch powder base made of matzoh meal and chicken fat.

* * *

LARGEST CHOPPED-LIVER MOLD

The world's largest chopped-liver mold was unveiled in Haifa at a ceremony commemorating the 25th anniversary of Israel independence. The giant 40- × 60- × 80-foot reproduction of Mt. Sinai was decorated with carved likenesses of Chaim Weitzman, David Ben-Gurion, Golda Meir, and Moshe Dayan. An interesting artistic touch was the 37-inch Moshe Dayan eye patch fashioned from a cluster of black olives.

OLDEST STAINED GLASS

The Bikar Golem Synagogue in Brussels, Belgium, at one time displayed a beautiful stained-glass window depicting in brilliant beet-red hues, the descent of Moses from Mt. Sinai. Supposedly dating back to the eleventh-century, it was a "must-see" tourist attraction for Jews right up to 1974, when a cleaning crew was hired to restore this historic attraction. While cleaning the stained-glass window with a strong detergent, the crew noticed that the colors had disappeared, leaving nothing but clear glass. An immediate investigation revealed that approximately 500 years before, during a holiday festival, a large quantity of borscht had been splashed onto the window.

In an effort to avoid disappointing the tourists, the entire cleanup crew spent the night splashing containers of borscht onto the windows in an attempt to recreate the original stained-glass illusion. They very nearly succeeded—until a careless workman shattered the entire window by failing to remove a boiled potato from the borscht.

CHAPTER 8

Mechanical Equipment

Telephones

LONGEST CALL

INDIVIDUAL

Shirley Rabinowitz of Port Washington, New York, carried on an uninterrupted conversation for 17 hours and 12 minutes before she discovered she had a wrong number.

GROUP

The longest telephone connection on record lasted 1500 hours, from March 6 to May 5, 1974, in the windup of a fund-raising campaign by the United Jewish Appeal. Volunteers worked one-hour shifts, talking steadily for 59½ days, soliciting funds for a medical center unit for the treatment of their laryngitis.

FASTEST TALKER

Yenta Lastfogel was clocked at a sustained average speaking speed of 43 words per second, when she spread the news to 17 neighbors in less than six minutes that her butcher, Chaim Lefkovitz, was cheating on his wife.

* * *

LONGEST WAIT

The longest wait on record for the telephone to ring was that of Mrs. Leyeh Adler, who spent 69 hours and 37 minutes sitting next to the phone, expecting a return call from her daughter, who had last said, "I'm busy now, Mom. I'll call you right back." This broke Mrs. Adler's previous record by 3 hours and 10 minutes, when she waited for a return call from her son, who had forgotten his mother's phone number.

* * *

FASTEST GOSSIP CENTER

The telephone company has established a special communications center in the Garden of Paradise Home for Retired Yentas in

Brooklyn, New York. To compensate for the residents' immobility due to infirmities, the company has installed a computerized "busybody" distribution center, which has the capacity of disseminating any given rumor to over 4000 neighbors within 2½ minutes. This new communication marvel is known as the *yentagram*.

* * *

ANSWERING SERVICE

The only answering service for *yentas* was started on February 14, 1977, by the Mount Vernon Chapter of the Jewish Federation of Women's Clubs. When the phone rings, a recorded message informs the caller that at the sound of the beep, she has 3 hours to leave a message, or 15 seconds to leave a rumor.

* * *

GREATEST NUMBER, PRIVATE HOME

The exclusive Scarsdale, New York, mansion of Mr. and Mrs. Manny Feitleman has a total of thirteen rotary set telephones, one for each room in the house, including the four bathrooms. Each phone is interconnected to the others with five rotary system lines and a "hold" button. In addition, the teenage daughter, Sabrina, has her own private Jewish

American Princess phone in her bedroom. Mr. Feitleman installed the system when he bought the house, in order to prevent family conflict over tying up the phone. Mrs. Feitleman, however, a busy club woman, manages to monopolize all five lines, pursuing activities with the True Sisters, the Hadassah, the Women's American ORT, the temple Sisterhood, the American Misrachi Women, and numerous other religious, social, and community involvements. So adroit is Mrs. Feitleman's manipulation of the "hold" button, that her husband hasn't used the phone in five years. Mr. Feitleman, a successful entrepreneur, uses the corner phone booth to conduct his bookmaking business.

Cars

FASTEST

The highest speed attained by any wheeled vehicle is 748.637 mph. The Israeli-designed vehicle called the "Silver Shnell" achieved this record during a secret test over a measured course in the Gaza Strip on November 13, 1976. Speculation that the car attained this incredible speed because of a nuclear-powered engine proved to be totally erroneous. The simple truth is that the speed of the "Silver Shnell" is due to the arrangement of the tires. It has two Arab tires in front and two Israeli tires in the back.

Planes

MOST NEIGHBORLY AIRLINE

The Israeli El Al Airlines has a reputation
for friendliness, hospitality, and making its
passengers feel at home unequaled by any
other international carrier. Every passenger
boarding the plane is offered "a piece fruit"
and is given a choice of sitting in one of two
sections—either in the Smoked Salmon section
or in the No Smoked Salmon section. Unlike
other airlines, which show movies, El Al has a
grandmotherly looking stewardess, who walks
up and down the aisle showing everybody pictures of her grandchildren.

*   *   *

MOST HAZARDOUS LANDING

On December 14, 1972, Captain Isaac Wein-
traub, the pilot of a Tel Aviv-bound El Al
Airlines flight carrying 102 passengers, lost
radio contact with the control tower as he
made his final approach. Unaware of the dense
fog on the ground, the captain had no hint of
the dangerous landing conditions until the last
possible moment. He knew he was in trouble
when he saw the runway lined with *yahrtzeit*
(memorial) candles.

CHAPTER 9

The Commercial World

Businesses

FASTEST EXPANSION

Isaac Cohen, a Russian immigrant who arrived in the United States at the depths of the big Depression of 1932, started with one pushcart of remnants on Hester Street on the lower East Side of New York City. With innate shrewdness and an intuitive merchandising sense, he expanded to 12 pushcarts within six months. One year later, Isaac opened his own six-story department store on the corner of Broadway and 33rd Street. The store has floor space of 250,000 square feet and contains more than 5,000 pushcarts.

MOST SUCCESSFUL VENTURE

In 1947, Irving Schwartzwalder, anticipating the United Nations vote to partition Palestine and form the state of Israel, negotiated, in perpetuity, a binding contract for the operation of the Kleenex concession at the Wailing Wall in Jerusalem.

*　　*　　*

WORST FAILURE

After working at menial jobs for 30 years in order to accumulate a nest egg and go into business for himself, Bernie "Shlemiel"* Wasserman invested his life savings in a franchise for a kosher delicatessen in Cairo, Egypt.

*　　*　　*

GREATEST GOING-OUT-OF-BUSINESS SALE

The greatest going-out-of-business sale ever held was at Ira Herzog's Clothing Emporium in Bremerton, Washington. The going-out-of-business sale, which began on July 11, 1929, is still going on.

* Foolish person; a sad sack; a dope.

SCHNORRERS (SCROUNGERS; MOOCHERS; BEGGARS)

RICHEST

Bainish Rothkovitz, a 64-year-old millionaire panhandler from Des Moines, Iowa, amassed a $4 million fortune by accepting all handouts on credit cards only.

BUSIEST

The busiest *schnorrer* on record is hard-working Moishe Carnovsky, age 63, of New York City. Over a period of 40 years, he built up a following on 7th Avenue between 14th Street and 42nd Street. But Moishe got so busy he was starting to fall behind in his panhandling schedule. He solved the problem when he took his son-in-law into the business and gave him the other side of the street.

* * *

PROSTITUTES

MOST HOSPITABLE

Dolly Adeleman, former *shadchen* (matchmaker), who is presently the owner and madam of San Francisco's most-successful bordello, is famous for the cordial manner in which she receives her customers. Every one of her extensive Jewish clientcle is welcomed at the door by Dolly herself with the warm, personal greeting, "Have I got a girl for you!"

Most Virtuous

Ida Greenbaum, age 38, of Sutton Place in Manhattan, New York, spent 13 profitable years at her profession, and still managed to retain her virginity, right up to the very day she found a successful Jewish customer who would marry her.

Most Charitable

Selma Sachs, owner and working madam of Beverly Hills' most-reputable bordello, is held in high esteem by her clientele, not so much for her professional know-how as for her philanthropy. This is not to imply that her services are given away *free*; her "fair-trade" prices are posted on each bedroom wall. But each bedroom, likewise, has several prominently labeled *pushkes* (Jewish piggy-banks) representing a wide range of Jewish charities. Clients are expected to distribute their loose change among these containers. Naturally, like any good American citizen, Selma writes off the totals collected under 'Contributions' at income tax time.

Employment

LONGEST

The longest recorded working career on one job is that of Morrie Mendelssohn of Rahway, New Jersey. He began his career as a chicken-flicker (plucker) in 1885 at the age of 15 for the Rabinowitz Happy Hen Poultry Farm. Morrie worked full time for 90 years until 1975, when he went into semiretirement. Today, at age 107, he still works at his trade part time. However, due to his advanced age and arthritis in his fingers, Morrie no longer plucks the chickens' feathers, he just loosens them.

SHORTEST

The shortest recorded working career was that of Max Feinstein of Los Angeles, California, who was employed as a sandwich man at Art's Delicatessen in North Hollywood. Feinstein, a Reformed Jew, started work November 5, 1977, at 7 A.M. and was fired at 7:05 the same morning when the boss caught him spreading mayonnaise on a bagel.

*   *   *

WAITERS

MOST DEVIOUS

Ziggy Ornstein, a 57-year-old waiter who has been working on the same job at the Moskewitz and Lupwitz restaurant for 32 years, still holds the world's record for going 18 consecutive weeks without allowing any customer to catch his eye.

MOST DISINTERESTED

Solly Wishnick, age 64, of the Bronx, New York, has been a waiter in a garment district coffee shop for the past 19 years. Solly holds the world's record for repeating 4,287 times, "Sorry, this ain't my table," despite the fact that Solly is the only waiter and there's only one table in the restaurant.

In his 53 years of waiting on tables in Factor's restaurant in Miami Beach, Max Zalkin has skillfully prevented every customer from ordering what he wanted on the menu and has, in every case, successfully touted the customer into ordering the leftover "Special of the day" that the restaurant is pushing. Even though he retired last month, Max still works as a technical advisor on a consulting basis three days a week.

Financial

TAXES, SHREWDEST WRITE-OFF

Successful tax accountant Eli Slotkin, whose education and business career had been financed by his father, Morris, refused his father's request for financial help, saying, "What have you done for me lately?" Just before he died, the impoverished Morris, in retribution, named his selfish son sole beneficiary to his bankrupt estate. Eli astutely made use of the bankrupt bequest as a tax loss.

CHARITIES

In the record-breaking time of three days, the Sisterhood of the King David Lodge of the Knights of Pythias raised over $30 million for the Jewish National Medical Research Foundation—enough money to enable the research team to justify starting a new disease.

MOST *Chutzpah* (UNMITIGATED NERVE)

The steering committee of the United Jewish Appeal, having set its fundraising goal by 1980 at a total of $1 billion, is sending the following notice to every contributor on its tremendous mailing list.

Dear Contributor:
Due to the increased cost of salaries, publications, travel expenses, campaigns, telethons, fund-raising dinners, lobbyists and a host of other inflationary factors, we are forced to raise the amount of your voluntary contributions by 30 percent for the coming year.

> Cordially,
> United Jewish Appeal

P.S. From the poverty-stricken, who cannot afford to make a contribution, we accept donation stamps.

Traditionally, Jews consider it a religious obligation to provide help to their *own* less fortunate and needy, and the number of Jewish organizations so engaged is steadily increasing. The fund-raising organization with the greatest number of causes is the United Jewish Consolidated Pushke Distribution Society. In an internationally coordinated fund-raising effort, the UJCPDS has raised funds for such worthy causes as:

- the Jewish Home for the Aged-Tall
- the Hebrew Yeshiva for Training Fund-Raisers
- the Hadassah Halfway House for Wayward Virgins
- the Jewish Memorial Hospital Wing for the Rehabilitation of Severe Whiplash Cases
- The Hebrew Rehabilitation Society for Defrocked Rabbis
- the Jewish Citizen's Common Cause Council to Protest Fund Raising
- the Jewish Asthmatic Hospital for Chicken-Pluckers Who Are Allergic to Feathers
- the Jewish Research Foundation for Curing Halvah Poisoning
- the Jewish Welfare League for the Distribution of Kosher Food Stamps to the Needy
- the Jewish Free Clinic for Low-Cholesterol Chicken Fat.

Ranches

LARGEST KOSHER CHICKEN RANCH

The largest kosher chicken ranch in the world
was the 7000-acre spread owned by Reb Lazarus Schulman, in Toms River, New Jersey.
To protect the kosher label and prevent
chicken rustling, Schulman decided to identify
every chicken with his own brand—the Lazy-
Gimmel-Circle-Aleph-Triangle-Baise-Bar-Dal-
od. Before the branding iron was applied,
Schulman's ranch had 2 million live chickens.
After the branding iron was applied, he had 2
million roasted chickens.

Real Estate

BARGAIN HUNTING

The family of Mr. and Mrs. Sam Horowitz of Newark, New Jersey, whose American ancestry has been traced back 350 years to the early settlers, holds the world's record for bargain hunting. Genealogical research has established that not a single member of the extensive Horowitz family tree has ever bought a single item at the retail price. This family practice started in 1626 with Jacob Horowitz, who was the first Horowitz to set foot in America. Jacob Horowitz acted as financial advisor to Peter Minuit, governor of the Dutch West India Company, in negotiating the purchase of Manhattan Island from the Indians. The retail price of the island was $130, but after a brief period of *hondling* (haggling), Horowitz made a final offer of $24 in beads and trinkets and bought the Island wholesale. It was later learned that the $24 in beads and trinkets cost Horowitz only $3 wholesale.

CHAPTER 10

The World of People

Medical

PHYSICIANS

MOST EXPENSIVE

Park Avenue doctor Louis Pransky, a 56-year-old respiratory specialist, is known to ask the highest fees in the world for his professional services. As an example of his price structure, his patients with walking pneumonia are charged by the mile.

MOST ORTHODOX

Dr. Saul Wasserman, an eminent eye, ear, nose, and throat specialist, has a practice consisting entirely of patients who observe strictly kosher dietary laws. In deference to his patients' religious needs, Dr. Wasserman conducts all of his examinations with two kinds of wooden tongue depressors—*milchedik* and *flayshig* (dairy and meat).

127

GREATEST NUMBER

The greatest concentration of Jewish doctors is found in New York City, on Central Park West between 59th and 72nd Streets, where a total of 27,000 doctors practice medicine. This is a ratio of 1 doctor for every 132 unmarried Jewish girls in the area.

OLDEST PRACTICING

Doctor Leon Klaubstein of Buffalo, New York, started practicing medicine in 1898. Today, at the age of 102, he still goes to his office every day to care for his one remaining patient—himself.

* * *

SYMPTOMS

MOST

The greatest number of medical symptoms in a single human being were found in Mrs. Sarah Grossinger, aged 69, a resident of the Mikvah Retirement Home in Chicago. Mrs. Grossinger can recite a list of more than 150 ailments, which include such complaints as headache, dizzy spells, blurred vision, stuffy nose, sore throat, fever, stiff neck, stomach cramps, dry skin, itching, backache, muscle spasm, hiccups, hot flashes, constipation, and gas. This is in reply to the routine question, "How are you?"

WORST HEARTBURN

The worst heartburn on record occurred on August 16, 1975, when Irwin Melnick of Bethpage, Long Island, foolishly drank too heavily and ate too much at his son's Bar Mitzvah party. The resulting heartburn was so severe that Mr. Melnick had to lie down while waiting for the doctor to arrive. In the interval, Mrs. Melnick, a gracious hostess, seized the opportunity to utilize the heartburn heat emanating from Mr. Melnick's chest as a hot tray to keep the knishes and cocktail franks warm.

WORST SIDE EFFECTS, PILLS

According to a recent survey of the Food and Drug Administration, Jewish girls between the ages of 14 and 19 are reported to suffer the worst incidence of side effects from taking birth control pills. The side effects—palpitations, fainting spells, and total collapse—do not effect the girls directly. They affect their Jewish mothers when they find out their daughters are taking the pills.

*　　*　　*

SURGERY, LARGEST GALLSTONE

The largest gallstone ever removed from a patient belonged to Chaim Gold of Brooklyn, New York. The gallstone was a perfectly formed rectangular slab measuring 8- × 4- × 1-inch thick. Mr. Gold did not survive the operation for obvious reasons, but his family, in fitting commemoration of their sad loss, had the gallstone inscribed and erected as a headstone.

*　　*　　*

COSMETIC SURGERY, MOST EXTENSIVE

On July 5, 1974, in Atlantic City, New Jersey, the most extensive cosmetic surgery ever attempted was performed on beauty contest hopeful Selma Schwartz, age 19. In a complex surgical procedure lasting 11 hours, a team of 15 plastic surgeons working simultaneously in three connecting operating rooms remodeled Selma's nose.

*　　*　　*

CIRCUMCISION

Most Novel

In order to support his family, Ira Feldman, age 49, a bartender at Lupowitz and Lupowitz Caterers in Spokane, Washington, supplements his income as a part-time *mohel* (circumciser). Influenced by bartending jargon, Ira conducts the circumcision ceremony by poising his medical instrument in the ready position and re-marking to the subject, "Say when!"

FASTEST

The world's fastest practitioner of the art of circumcision is Dr. Seymour Grunbaum, resident *mohel* of the Young Israel Maternity Hospital in Minneapolis. Bypassing all traditional medical techniques in the circumcision procedure, Dr. Grubaum has successfully performed as many as 250 circumcisions in a single day by using a pencil sharpener.

* * *

MENTAL HEALTH

EARLIEST NERVOUS BREAKDOWN

The earliest record of a nervous breakdown occurred, according to the Scriptures, during the period of King Solomon's reign (circa 1000 B.C.). At the peak of power and prosperity in his kingdom, King Solomon's self-indulgence proved to be his undoing. There was a noticeable deterioration in Solomon's control of his own destiny, when he filled his harem with 1000 wives. This put him under such severe daily stress that he began to suffer chronic anxiety neurosis due to acute nagging.

LATEST PSYCHOTHERAPY

Remarkable strides are being made in the Jewish Advanced Mental Health Center in Denver, Colorado, where the use of bold new clinical techniques are achieving amazing psychotherapeutic results. Jewish mothers suffering from anxiety, depression, and palpitations are responding rapidly to treatment in the new Aggravation Wing. The program features such therapeutic devices as:

- Three tape-recorded telephone calls a day from the children.
- At least once a day a tall, handsome surrogate son-in-law walks in the room and says, "Hello, Mom."
- Each mother daily is shown a list of medical complaints, from which she is permitted to select her very own "Symptom of the Day."
- Biweekly classes in guilt inducement.
- Daily domination calisthenics.

NEWEST CHILDREN'S INSTITUTE

Advanced clinical behavioral science studies of anxiety neurosis among Jewish children currently constitutes the major thrust of the psychiatric research program conducted by the entire staff of the brand-new Cedars of Guilt Hospital in Bayonne, New Jersey.

HOSPITALS, LONGEST STAY

Hannah Fishman of Beverly Hills, California, age 32 and unmarried, had herself admitted to Cedars-Sinai Hospital in Los Angeles, where she stayed on as a patient for 16 years, hoping to catch an eligible doctor.

Law

BIGGEST LAWSUIT

The highest damages ever sought were $2½ billion from the city of Los Angeles, following the disastrous 1971 earthquake. The sum was requested in a class-action suit filed for personal injuries on behalf of the entire Jewish population of Los Angeles, which claimed whiplash.

* * *

LONGEST TRIAL

In Tiberias, Israel, the longest trial ever recorded was a divorce action (Yetta vs. Herman Solomon), lasting 42 days. The jury deliberated for an additional 53 days without reaching a verdict. Judge Lazarus Lipkin was forced to declare a mistrial after the foreman reported that the jury was deadlocked at eight guilty, one not guilty, and three who didn't want to mix in.

*   *   *

LAWYER, BIGGEST *SHLIMAZLE* (BORN LOSER)

Harry Tarnofsky, who took the Minnesota State Bar exam 21 times, finally passed in 1956. He then practiced law for 18 years without acquiring a single client. In sheer desperation, Mr. Tarnofsky filed suit for divorce against his own wife so he would have at least one case before he retired. He lost the case.

*   *   *

LONGEST WILL

The longest will on record was that of Sidney Schwartz of Brooklyn, New York, who died at age 92. His last will and testament consisted of 15 bound volumes, containing over 1 million words. The relatives to whom bequests were made never benefited because they all died from old age during the reading of the will.

MOST MYSTIFYING APPEAL

On June 8, 1975, Morris Goldstein, 32, of Astoria, Long Island, on trial for burglary, heard the jury deliver a verdict pronouncing him innocent. He immediately had his attorney file an appeal to reverse the jury's verdict on the grounds that the presence of three elderly Jewish mothers on the jury made him feel guilty.

Crime and Punishment

ROBBERY

JEWELS

The largest jewel robbery on record occurred on August 14, 1974 in Seigleman's Diamond Salon in the New York Diamond Mart on 44th Street. In less than a minute, a three-member gang snatched an incalculable fortune in uncut stones and would have gotten away cleanly if they hadn't waited around for an appraisal.

BANKS, MOST *Chutzpah* (UNMITIGATED GALL)

On June 8, 1973, Arnie Margolen, age 32, single-handedly robbed the Lipkin Commercial Trust and Savings Bank in Phoenix, Arizona. Margolen got away with $30,000 in cash and immediately stepped over to the new-accounts department, where he opened up a savings account.

MOST STOLEN CREDIT CARDS

The most credit cards ever stolen—57—were taken on January 12, 1974, in Saks Fifth Avenue. They belonged to Mrs. Brenda Beilowitz of Queens, New York. Her husband never reported the theft because the thief was buying less than his wife.

* * *

CLEVEREST PETTY THIEF

Jacob Teitlebaum, age 52, of New York City, frequented Gluckstern's Kosher Cafeteria in mid-Manhattan and sewed leak-proof rubber pockets in his pants so he could steal matzohball soup.

* * *

GREATEST SHOPLIFTER

Mimi Moscowitz, age 57, of the Bronx, New York, has been arrested 137 times for shoplifting. Each arrest was for stealing from somebody's pushcart on Delancy Street in New York City's Lower East Side. When asked why she only shoplifted from Delancy Street pushcarts, Mrs. Moscowitz replied, "Where else can you find such bargains?"

GREATEST FOILED ROBBERY

The greatest foiled robbery on record occurred on August 14, 1968, at the First National Bank of Tel Aviv. The perfectly plotted and flawlessly synchronized holdup was attempted by a gang of 12 militant Orthodox dissidents, who almost got away with over $6 million in loot. The robbery failed and the gang was apprehended when its leader, Moishe Doberman, disrupted the split-second timing of the operation by stopping to kiss the *mezuzah* as he was leaving the bank.

*   *   *

MURDERS, MOST UNSOLVED

At the peak of the gang murders in the late thirties, in the Brownsville section of Brooklyn, New York, there were 97 unsolved murders in one month. The most notorious was the disappearance of Buggsy Bialystok, who was paid protection by all the synagogues in Brooklyn. It was rumored that a contract was put out by Sol and Bernie Scholsberg, the famous Twin Cantors. The hit man encased Buggsy's feet in two huge potato knishes and dumped him into Sheepshead Bay. Although the body was never recovered, an epidemic of dead fish floating on the surface of Sheepshead Bay provided a clue to the disappearance, when the Brooklyn coroner determined that all the fish had died from aggravated heartburn.

EMBEZZLEMENT, SNEAKIEST

Muttle Goldfarb, a 52-year-old teller at the First Pincus Savings Bank of Saint Paul, Minnesota, over a period of 15 years carried out a plan of embezzlement by daily swallowing coins. At the time of his death on October 3, 1973, an autopsy was performed to determine why he weighed more than 600 pounds. Only at that point was it discovered that Muttle had swallowed a total of $15,247.23 in silver dollars, half dollars, quarters, dimes, nickels, and pennies, plus $173.81 in interest compounded daily.

* * *

SWINDLE, GREATEST

The greatest swindle ever was perpetrated in Bloomington, Illinois, by Solly "The Goniff"* Liebowitz who, during the Passover holidays in 1973 made more than $300,000 by passing counterfeit "Kosher-for-Pesach"† Manischewitz matzohs.

* * *

PAYOFF, LONGEST

Over a period of 45 years on the Philadelphia Police Force, Detective Sergeant Sol Kaplan received a total of $225,000 in illicit bribes.

* Thief; robber.   † Passover.

He averaged $5000 a year in payoffs right up to the day of his mandatory retirement at age 65, when he was able to retire on half-graft.

* * *

EXTORTIONIST, MOST SUCCESSFUL

The most successful extortionist on record is Jake "The Syringe" Plotkin, who in 1973 personally siphoned off an estimated $10 million from more than 3000 wealthy Jews, without arrest or prosecution. Pulling out all the stops, Plotkin used fear, intimidation, veiled threats, social manipulation, moral blackmail, and guilt on his "marks" to become the most successful fund raiser in the history of the United Jewish Appeal.

* * *

SUICIDE

Most Talkative

On October 3, 1976, Mrs. Dora Teitlebaum, age 57, of New York City, an incorrigible *yenta,* leaped from the top of the 121-story World Trade Center in Manhattan. "Yenta" Teitlebaum lived to tell about it. She told it to the people on the 80th floor. She told it to the people on the 60th floor. She told it to the people on the 40th floor, the 20th floor, and all the way down.

Most Considerate

Mrs. Rosalie Rothenberg of Las Vegas, Nevada, age 47, despondent over the fact that her beloved husband, a pit boss at the Grand Motel Casino, was chasing around with a cocktail waitress, decided to end it all by sticking her head in the oven. At the same time, she put in a pot roast so her husband should have something to eat when he came home.

Most Vain

Sophie Silverman, age 39, of Margate, Florida, depressed over her 350 pound obesity problem, attempted to commit suicide by swallowing 30 pounds of saccharine and taking a large overdose of diet pills, so she would look thin and attractive when they found the body.

* * *

PRISON, LAST MEAL

Longest

The longest last meal ever served to a condemned Jewish convict was that of Abe Hershkowitz, long-time resident of Death Row, Sing Sing. His mother, Reba Hershkowitz, concerned about her son's health, had obtained special permission from the warden to prepare and serve her son's last meal. Like any good

Jewish mother, Mrs. Hershkowitz cooked all of her son's favorite dishes. In order for Abe to finish his last meal, the governor had to grant six reprieves.

Worst Service

Herschel Pasternak, age 42, was scheduled to die on August 18, 1973, for killing five waiters in a Tel Aviv restaurant. His execution had to be delayed for three days because every time he asked a passing guard to order his last meal, the guard replied nervously, "I'm sorry, sir, but this isn't my cell."

Religion

SYNAGOGUES

MOST REFORMED

The Free-Thinkers Temple of Kalamazoo, Michigan, boasts 234 nonreligious activities in which members of the congregation are encouraged to participate. Numbered among these are such progressive programs as the:

- Sisterhood of the Chauvinist Men's Club
- Yiddish Literary Forum and Athletic League
- Arbitman Reading Circle and Tennis for Israel Group
- Ladies' Jewish Defense League Mah Jong Society
- Jewish Women's Liberation Bridge Club

- Sons and Daughters of Israel Gin Rummy Team
- Jewish Parents' Child-Overindulgence Study Group
- Mothers of Israel Guilt-Advisory Council
- Daughters of Israel Pill-Advisory Committee
- Anti-Defamation League Summer Camp Basic Training Center
- Rabbi Evaluation Encounter Group
- Free-Thinkers' Temple Dybbuk Exorcism Committee
- Temple Neighborhood Golem Watch Wardens
- Interfaith Compulsory Busing Program

And of course there is the

- Militant "No-More-Religious-Services" Pro-est Marchers.

The Free-Thinkers' Temple, moreover, provides such innovative features as "Rapid-Pray Religious Services" at its Drive-In-Worship-Window, conducted entirely in English.

MOST APPROPRIATE NAME

The most suitable name of a synagogue is that of a Reformed temple in Shirley, Long Island, known as Shirley Temple. There is absolutely no truth to the allegation that included in the Shirley Temple Choir's repertoire of religious psalms is the song "On the Good Ship Lollypop."

RITUAL, LONGEST CEREMONY

The longest ritual ceremony was a Passover Seder (service) in 1933 at the home of Reb Aaron Schlepperman. The Seder lasted 9 hours and 33 minutes and was followed by the discovery that, out of the 47 assembled guests, 13 adults had fainted and 9 children were suffering from malnutrition.

* * *

PRAYERS, FIRST TELEVISED

The first televised prayers took place at the Galilee Stadium in Israel on August 7, 1957, prior to an international soccer match. For those who missed the highlights of the opening benediction, the station telecast an instant repray.

* * *

SINNER, MOST REPENTANT

The most repentant sinner was wealthy Orthodox Jew Julius Berkovitz, who in 1931 spent the entire Yom Kippur holiday at the Beth Olam Synagogue in Gary, Indiana, in continuous fasting and prayer for the atonement of his sins during the previous year. In beseeching forgiveness, the physical demands of uninterrupted prayer and rending of garments were so intense that Mr. Berkovitz wore out three *tallises* (prayer shawls), and four *yamulkes* (skull caps), and cracked two of his ribs from breast-beating. The following day, feeling cleansed of his sins, he started out the new year by foreclosing the mortgage of the synagogue.

*　*　*

YARMULKE, SMALLEST

The smallest *yarmulke* in existence is a 1/16-inch black bead used daily by a praying mantis converted to Judaism.

Funerals

THRIFTIEST

In order to get his money's worth out of his funeral, Irving Ploppman, age 72, of St. Louis, Missouri, requested that he be ̇cremated and his ashes saved in an urn until winter, when the ashes were to be scattered over the icy sidewalk in front of his house.

*   *   *

MOST OSTENTATIOUS

In compliance with the wishes of his deceased wife, Sadie, Meyer Horwitz of Miami Beach, Florida, arranged to have her laid to rest seated in her metallic-gold Cadillac Sedan de Ville, outfitted in her full-length, natural-mink coat over a sequined décolleté formal evening gown. Her diamond rings, diamond pendant, and sapphire earrings were complemented by a new permanent and a bouffant hairdo. The final resting place of the Cadillac is by a parking meter adjacent to the entrance of the Fountainbleau Hotel. Her considerate husband has arranged for perpetual parking-meter care, with hired personnel inserting a dime every hour on the hour.

* * *

LONGEST DELAYED

Traditionally, religious Jews are buried within 24 hours of death. Sam Weisman, however, age 55, of Philadelphia, who dropped dead in the lobby of the Concord Hotel in the Catskills as he was signing the guest register, was not buried until his two-week vacation was over.

* * *

EULOGY, MOST PUZZLING

The most puzzling eulogy ever delivered was given on May 17, 1974, at the funeral of Melvin "The Momzer"* Markowitz. The funeral was attended by only eleven people because Markowitz, although from a very large family, was the most detested and despised relative of them all. The eulogy was delivered by Rabbi

---

* Hard-hearted ogre; slave driver; bill collector; landlord.

Simon Feldman, a last-minute substitute and a stranger to the Markowitz family. Rabbi Feldman described the deceased in such glowing terms that all eleven mourners, including five members of the immediate family, walked out in the middle of the eulogy, thinking they were at the wrong funeral.

*　　*　　*

MOURNING PERIOD, SHORTEST

After 25 years of marriage, Mrs. Velma Feigler of Forest Hills, New York, buried her deceased husband, March 9, 1977. Forgoing the traditional waiting period before unveiling the grave marker, Mrs. Feigler had the bronze plaque inscribed and put in place two days later. The epitaph read:

TO MY BELOVED
IRA FEIGLER

BORN 1923—DIED 1977

LEAVING HIS WIDOW, VELMA,
WHO IS LOOKING FOR A NICE
YOUNG MAN.

TELEPHONE 555-8765

CEMETERIES, MOST EXCLUSIVE

The new Beverly Hills Jewish Memorial Park is the most exclusive in the world. It is also the most expensive, catering only to those dead who can afford it. The high value of Beverly Hills property is reflected in the price of the cemetery plots, which start at $5000 per individual plot and $50,000 and up per family plot. These prices do *not* include the cost of the casket, use of the chapel, funeral services, the rabbi's services, the funeral coach, the limousine, the opening and closing of the grave, and *paid* honorary pallbearers. Since 'exclusiveness' is the hallmark of the Beverly Hills Jewish Memorial Park, for those deceased wishing privacy, there is no extra charge for unlisted tombstones.

Military and Defense

LONGEST

The longest war in Jewish history was the continuing Biblical conflict between the ancient Hebrews and the Syrians, which lasted from 516 to 165 B.C. Historians named it the "298-Year War." Actually, the war lasted almost 350 years, but the Hebrews marked it down to 298.

SHORTEST, RENAISSANCE:

On April 12, 1475, the Jews living in the Minsk ghetto revolted against their Russian oppressors. The revolt started late Friday afternoon and ended 33 minutes later, when the Jews couldn't find any *goyem* (gentiles) to light the cannons after sundown.

SHORTEST, MODERN

The shortest modern war ever recorded was the 1967 six-day conflict between the Arabs and Israel. The swiftness of the Israeli victory was no accident; it was part of the Israeli military's master strategy. The Israel's had to win the war in less than seven days because all the Israeli military equipment was rented by the week.

COSTLIEST

The most expensive Jewish war was the 1967 Israeli-Arab conflict. Despite the fact that the war lasted only six days, the Israeli government spent more than $900 million, of which $670 million went for accounting fees.

MILITARY STRATEGY, WORST TACTICAL COMMAND

After Moses and his exhausted, hungry followers paused at the shores of the Red Sea to eat a hasty meal, Moses proceeded to part the waters. Although hotly pursued by the Egyptian soldiers, Moses commanded his nervous people to wait for two hours after eating before attempting to cross the Red Sea, so they shouldn't get stomach cramps.

Food

MATZOH BALL, LARGEST

At the Manischewitz Matzoh-Ball Bake-Off held annually at Grossingers, New York, Mrs. Lillian Schlefstein of Mount Vernon was declared the blue-ribbon winner in the giant-size event. Setting a new world record for massiveness, Mrs. Schlefstein's matzoh ball measured 15 feet, 8 inches in diameter and weighed 1201 pounds. Unfortunately, before the official awards presentation, Mrs. Schlefstein was disqualified when it was discovered that her monumental matzoh ball had been injected with silicone.

CHICKEN SOUP, LARGEST AMOUNT

The greatest quantity of chicken soup ever prepared at one time contained 45,000 gallons of water, 3000 fresh-killed kosher hens (plucked by a corps of 30 master chicken-flickers), 300 pounds of salt, 2 box cars of soup-'n'-greens, and 2 million pounds of noodles (which laid end to end would encircle the earth nine times). All of these ingredients were cooked in the Israeli government's Olympic-size heated swimming pool, located at the new training camp in the Sinai Desert. It took 40 days and 40 nights to cook the soup, but the coaches of the Israeli swimming team were convinced that their athletes would not only benefit from the nutritional value of unlimited chicken soup at the training table, but would, in addition, be able to achieve their peak physical condition in time for Olympic competition, by swimming in it.

* * *

RECIPES, OLDEST

The oldest known surviving written recipe, dated 1487, was found in a *mezuzah* belonging to the Shapiro family in Spokane, Washington, in September 1974. This 487-year-old family recipe, called "Tsimmes Rachmones Surprise" (Pitiful Pudding Surprise) contained chicken *schmaltz*, fresh-ground horseradish, pepper corns, raw onions, *gribbiness* (cracklings), crushed garlic cloves, *kasha* (grits), and stale bread. According to family tradition, this recipe was handed down at deathbed from mother to daughter, for 11 consecutive generations. While the recipe still survives, the people who eat it don't.

*   *   *

HEALTHIEST

Mrs. Freda Poliakoff, a dietician in the Jewish Memorial Hospital of Lincoln, Nebraska, has developed many special recipes. She is best known for her *gefilte helzel* (stuffed chicken neck). Mrs. Poliakoff's secret lies in the fact that instead of using ordinary thread to sew both ends of the neck, she does it with dental floss. This enables the patients to eat and clean their teeth at the same time.

CHAPTER 11

Human
Accomplishments

Marriage and Divorce

MOTHERS

MOST DESPERATE

The most desperate mother on record is Mrs. Miriam Mendleson, a wealthy 56-year-old widow of Cleveland, Ohio, who lives with her 34-year-old unmarried daughter, Diane. While mailing a letter at the local post office, Mrs. Mendleson saw an FBI poster that offered a $50,000 reward for information leading to the whereabouts of the ten most-wanted men. With her unmarried daughter in mind, Mrs. Mendleson immediately posted a notice announcing her own offer of $100,000 for information leading to the whereabouts of the ten most-wanted men.

On September 9, 1976, Mrs. Sylvia Shorr and her unmarried daughter, Phyliss, age 47, were shopping in downtown Topeka, Kansas. As they passed the First Federal Bank, a robber dashed from the entrance and grabbed Phyliss from behind, holding her as a hostage. Seeing her daughter held in a viselike grip by a young man, Mrs. Shorr seized the opportunity to dash madly into a nearby stationary store and order 50 engagement announcements.

* * *

ENGAGEMENT, LONGEST

The longest engagement on record lasted 12 years. Dr. Alvin Kooperman, age 32, and Bernice Goodman, age 29, announced their engagement on July 18, 1964, when Dr. Kooperman promised Bernice that they would be married as soon as he started earning enough money to support a wife. After 12 years of waiting, Bernice's patience ran out, and she broke their engagement. The rejected Dr. Kooperman immediately asked her to return the engagement ring, after which he sent her a bill for 2752 house calls.

WEDDING ANNOUNCEMENTS, MOST ECSTATIC

When their 42-year-old daughter, Zelda, finally received a proposal of marriage, her joyous parents, Mr. and Mrs. Baruch Zimmerman of Salt Lake City, Utah, sent out the following wedding announcement:

Mr. and Mrs. Baruch Zimmerman
are
greatly relieved
to
announce the marriage
of their single
daughter
Zelda
to
somebody

*   *   *

WEDDINGS, ANGRIEST

The angriest wedding on record took place at Lupowitz Catering Hall in Cleveland, Ohio, on December 11, 1968, after all of the invited relatives received their seating place cards and found out which other relatives were seated at the same table.

BRIDE AND BRIDEGROOM, OLDEST

The oldest bride and bridegroom on record are Rivka Doffstein, 101, and Herman Skulnick, 103, who were married on June 12, 1974. The highlight of the wedding reception was a Viennese table displaying a gigantic pulsating, heart-shaped Jello mold with a genuine pacemaker in it.

* * *

MARRIAGES

LONGEST

On March 10, 1977, Ephraim Scheinheim (age 100) and his wife, Deborah (age 96), were honored for their 80th wedding anniversary by a gathering in Philadelphia of more than 250 relatives. When called upon to toast this event, Mr. Scheinheim raised a glass of wine nostalgically and said, "It is wonderful to have so many near and dear ones here with us to commemorate this day. I have been married to my beloved wife, Deborah, for 80 relentless years, and I hope that the next time all of us get together, it will be on a *happy* occasion."

For all of the 63 years of their married life, Mr. and Mrs. Izzy Margulies of Castro Valley, California, abhorred and detested one another. Nevertheless, they stayed married anyway, because of the children, the grandchildren, the great-grand-children, and the great-great-grandchildren.

* * *

WEDDING GIFTS, FASTEST EX-CHANGE

Mrs. Sylvia Fish, age 35, of San Francisco, has been married fifteen times and holds the world's record for exchanging more than 4700 wedding gifts within a two-year period. She also holds the world's record within the same two-year period for exchanging seven husbands.

Wealth and Poverty

MOST MISERLY MAN

Tight-fisted Sol Plotkin, a wealthy clothing manufacturer in Pittsburgh, Pennsylvania, has for years resisted all pleas from Jewish charitable organizations for financial contributions. In 1976, when asked to contribute something to the Jewish Home for the Aged, he relented and sent his mother and father.

* * *

POOREST FAMILY

The poverty-stricken Max Silverbaums of Richmond, Virginia, who have four children, a grandfather, and two boarders, have been evicted so often that Mrs. Silverbaum has had plastic covers made for the street lamps.

GREATEST RECLUSE

The Kollyika brothers, Abe and Jules, twin re-
cluses (1897–1964), lived a totally isolated
life in the teeming Brownsville section of
Brooklyn, New York. Secluded in a one-room
basement apartment, they emerged only at
night, through a crawl-hole into the alley, to
scavenge for food. Unshaven, dressed in rags,
and living amid tons of junk collected over a
period of 50 years, it is not surprising that the
rumor spread concerning great hidden wealth.
On August 9, 1964, the Kollyikas's apartment
was broken into by two prowlers, who mur-
dered the brothers and ripped open their
mattress to find it contained over $25 million
in pledges.

Endurance

MOTHERS-IN-LAW

LONGEST STAY

Ignoring her husband's fierce objections, Becky Lipsky invited her mother to live with them. Her mother, Mrs. Goldie Wolf, arrived August 2 hours and 42 minutes of her first visit to her there, despite the fact that Mrs. Wolf dropped dead the very day of her arrival in 1932. Mindful of his wife's grief, and in an effort to assuage her guilt over the unfulfilled promise that her now-deceased mother could live with them, husband Max, a taxidermist, had his mother-in-law stuffed and mounted in the guest room.

Mrs. Sophie Seigal of Riverdale, New York, in keeping with the traditional belief that "no girl is good enough for my son," compiled a record-breaking list of 110 complaints in the 2 hours and 42 minutes of her first visit to her son and daughter-in-law's house, the day they returned from their honeymoon. The complaints covered a broad spectrum of hostilities on the subject of:

Subject	Number	Examples
Cleaning	32	Bed wasn't made. Dirty toilet bowls. Dishes in the sink.
Clothing	18	Spends every nickel on clothes. My son wears rags.
Cooking	26	All she knows is opening a can. Her coffee is poison. Dreck she cooks. The refrigerator is empty.
Hospitality	15	She never offered me a glass of water. We sat in the kitchen. She didn't get off the phone. She didn't ask me to stay for dinner.

Health	9	She smokes like a chimney.
		My son looks like a skeleton.
		She wouldn't even turn on the heat.
Personal Habits	10	Didn't get dressed all day.
		Never combs her hair.
		Never uses makeup.

Total Complaints 110

Mrs. Seigal's list of complaints is so comprehensive that she has published a completely cross-indexed guide of complaints, which she sells to new mothers-in-law as a basic training manual. This service includes a weekly newsletter updating the latest complaints.

*   *   *

GRANDMOTHERS

CARRIAGE PUSHING

The longest continuous baby-carriage-pushing record is held by Sophie Gutterman, a 76-year-old Bronx grandmother. She pushed her grandson's carriage for a record 83 miles in 42 consecutive hours, until every one of the 4327 neighbors in the immediate vicinity had seen her grandson at least twice. She then proceeded to break the world's carriage-pushing *speed* record by pursuing a reluctant stranger down the busy Grand Concourse at

37 mph. She was finally apprehended by a policeman who issued her a citation for reckless carriage pushing.

Kvelling (TO BEAM WITH IMMENSE PRIDE AND PLEASURE)

The *kvelling* (feeling proud) record was established on July 15, 1971, in Boston, by a brand-new grandmother, Esther Schkulnick, age 59. During a nine-hour period she proudly recited a nonstop stream of more than 4200 traditional phrases complimentary to her new grandson. These included, but were not limited to, the following:

"You think *he's* cute—you should see his pictures."

"He's such a darling. Sleeps like a baby."

"In *your life* did you ever see such a child?"

"Look at those lashes. A girl he should've been."

"Such a smart boy. He takes after my son."

"You could eat him up."

"He looks exactly like my Hymie, may he rest in peace."

"Did you ever see such a healthy baby?"

"Look at that smile. You could die from it."

Mrs. Schkulnick would have broken her own record if the baby hadn't vomited all over her, ending her achievement with the proud exclamation: "Oy, has that baby got a mouth on him!"

* * *

MARATHON FLOOR SCRUBBING

The world's record for continuous floorscrubbing is held by Mrs. Gittle Applebaum of Boston. In preparation for the Passover holidays in 1972, Mrs. Applebaum scrubbed her 10- × 10-foot linoleum kitchen floor for 264 consecutive hours, or a total of 11 days. As a result of her marathon scrubbing effort, Mrs. Applebaum was unable to serve the Passover dinner because her hand couldn't be pried loose from the scrub brush.

* * *

NONSTOP TALKING

At the annual Yenta-Thon held June 12, 1974, in Coney Island, Mrs. Fruma Hirsch of Brooklyn, New York, on the verge of breaking the existing nonstop talking record of 245 hours and 10 minutes, collapsed breathlessly and was administered emergency oxygen in the ambulance on the way to the hospital. This enabled her to keep talking even after she was admitted to the hospital and put in intensive care, where she continued talking for another 37 hours until she lapsed into a coma. This still did not prevent Mrs. Hirsch from talking another 18 hours, up to the very minute she expired. Nevertheless, Mrs. Hirsch went on to establish an incredible nonstop talking record of 342 hours and 18 minutes, when the emergency medical team immediately attached life-support machines to her tongue.

Miscellaneous Endeavors

MOST CLOTHING

In January of 1973, during a snow storm in New York City, Mrs. Dora Weiskoff, an over-protective mother, set a new record for the most clothing ever worn, by dressing her seven-year-old son, Barry, warmly "so he shouldn't catch a cold playing in the snow." She dressed the boy in two T-shirts and a pair of boxer shorts, over which she put two sets of long underwear. She covered his feet and legs with three pairs of heavy, woolen knee-length stockings and two pairs of corduroy pants. She protected his body with a woolen lumberjack shirt, a sweat shirt, and three woolen sweaters. Over his feet she placed fleece-lined boots covered by a pair of her own galoshes. She then wrapped a 12-foot scarf around his neck and across his chest, holding it in place with a windbreaker and two woolen jackets. A ski mask, ear muffs, and a fur-lined leather hat were tied down by a heavy woolen muffler. Over a pair of heavy-duty, fur-lined gloves, she placed a set of mittens. The entire outfit was held firmly in place by a belted, interlined overcoat. By the time she got him dressed for the winter snow, it was the first day of spring, so Mrs. Weiskoff had to undress her son. As the very last piece of clothing was removed, it was winter again. Today, at the age of 11, Barry Weiskoff has not been out of the house in four years.

* * *

SYMPATHETIC PHRASES, GREATEST NUMBER

The world's record for the greatest number of sympathetic phrases uttered belongs to Mrs. Vanessa Grubschmidt of Moshulo Parkway, Bronx, New York. On April 4, 1969, over a cup of coffee, Mrs. Grubschmidt managed to interject a total of 1264 sympathetic responses during a 22-minute recitation, in minute detail by her neighbor, Mrs. Goldblatt about her recent hysterectomy. Among Mrs. Grubschmidt's compassionate responses were such understanding phrases as:

- *Oy!* (Oy!)
- *Oy vay iz mir!* (Woe is me!)
- *Gevalt!* (Oy!)
- *Hoo Hah!* (Hoo hah!)
- *Ein kleinikite!* (Big deal!)
- *Halevai!* (I hope so!)
- *Gottenyu!* (Dear God!)
- *Oy, tsuris!* (What troubles!)
- *A metsieh!* (A bargain!)
- *Kein ein ahorrgh!* (Knock on wood!)
- *Oy, schlecht!* (That's bad!)

Mrs. Goldblatt was so overwhelmed by her neighbor's sympathetic understanding, she immediately made an appointment with her doctor for another surgery she didn't even need.

* * *

BAR MITZVAH

LARGEST

The largest Bar Mitzvah on record took place on February 15, 1973, on the 600,000-acre ranch of cattle baron Yankel "Tex" Rosenblatt. Honoring his Bar Mitzvah boy, Velvel, the affair was attended by more than

4000 invited guests and featured a gargantuan outdoor Texas-style barbecue. Forty-two of rancher Rosenblatt's prize kosher longhorns, weighing 84,000 pounds dressed, were impaled end to end on a giant rotisserie with a spit measuring 90 feet in length. At the end of the 26-hour roast, the barbecued meat was diced and served to the assembled guests on 450 million Ritz crackers.

MOST EXOTIC

On April 9, 1977, Mr. and Mrs. Abe Mintz booked the banquet facilities of Temple B'nai Jacob in Reseda, California, to celebrate the Bar Mitzvah of their son, Larry. For this occasion the entire banquet hall was redecorated to reflect an African jungle motif, and the room was appropriately renamed "B'nai Zulu" for the evening. The decor was highlighted by a backdrop of dense jungle undergrowth, chattering monkeys, a champagne fountain bubbling up out of a quicksand swamp in a humid temperature of 102 degrees, for an authentic jungle background. The party would have been a huge success except for the fact that the realistic jungle atmosphere caused two nieces and a great-uncle to contract malaria, the Bar Mitzvah boy to get swamp fever, and the chopped-liver mold to develop a bad case of jungle rot.

Gastronomic Records

MOST FOOD EATEN

The greatest intake of food at one meal was accomplished by Boris Steinberg on January 4, 1953. He consumed 6 quarts of chicken soup, 17 matzoh balls, 5 pounds of chopped liver, 9 pounds of *flanken,* and 8 pineapple cheesecakes. He washed it all down with 32 glasses of tea, encouraged in his record-breaking feat by his mother, who kept repeating, "Eat. Eat. There are children starving in India."

CARBONATED BEVERAGES

On August 23, 1973, Abe Lowenstein of Huntington, Long Island, while attending a family-circle picnic at Jones Beach, consumed a record 102 cases of Dr. Brown's Celery Tonic and 208 bottles of seltzer which amounted to an intake of 4 million cubic feet of gas in a single afternoon. The next day Mr. Lowenstein was officially certified by the Department of Interior as the fourth-largest untapped natural gas reserve in the United States. Today, as an emergency energy measure, Mr. Lowenstein is hooked up to a pipeline in Texas.

* * *

SALAMI

At the annual Nosh-A-Rama Championships held at Yankee Stadium in the Bronx on July 16, 1972, a total of 25 four-man teams from all over the world qualified for the final event—the "Hundred-Yard Salami-Nosh Dash." A 150-foot salami, weighing 700 pounds and with a 20-inch circumference, was devoured by the Young Maccabee team in the record-breaking time of 17 minutes and 32 seconds. The team was disqualified, however, when the required saliva test revealed that two members of the team had broken the rules by eating a full meal just before the final event.

SUGAR SUCKING

The ritual art of prolonging the longevity of a sugar cube (held between one's teeth) while sipping a glass of tea reached its highest level of refinement in Russia during the Czarist regime, when sugar cubes were a very scarce delicacy among the impoverished Jews in the Russian *shtetlach* (villages). The record for sugar sucking was held by Schmilke Yanovitch of Finster-Gubernia, who started a fresh cube of sugar in December 1887, and used it continuously for almost nine years and more than 8300 glasses of tea, right up to 1896 when he died from diabetes.

Homemakers

THRIFTIEST

The record for stretching the household dollar is held by Sylvia Portnoy of Gary, Indiana, who in 1977 spent only $2000 out of an $8000 household allowance, thereby saving $6000. Her creative cooking economizing helped win the battle against inflation. For example, Mrs. Portnoy saved $1643 on her meat bill alone with such inventive methods as cooking her brisket of beef in Woolite to keep it from shrinking.

ROOM SHOWING

Mrs. Gertrude Feldman, who has been living in the same house in Detroit, Michigan, for the past 18 years, has just broken the world's room-showing record. During this period, Mrs. Feldman has conducted a total of 1323 guided tours through every room in the house for visiting friends and relatives. Averaging four persons per tour, she has shown the house to more than 5000 people. Mrs. Feldman's room-showing habit has become so deeply ingrained that on March 8, 1977, at 3 A.M., when a burglar broke in, she compulsively showed him through every room in the house except the master bedroom which she omitted because the bed wasn't made.

* * *

CLEANEST KITCHEN

The cleanest Jewish kitchen in the world is in the home of Mr. and Mrs. Manny Feinberg, who live with their seven children in an apartment on Pelham Parkway, Bronx, New York. In order not to leave any crumbs, this family of nine eats all of its meals over the kitchen sink. For formal entertaining the sink can be extended to accommodate as many as 20 people.

DUSTING

The world speed record for dusting a 3000-square-foot house, including all the furniture and accessories, belongs to Mrs. Dora "Dustin'" Hoffman of Mt. Vernon, New York. Mrs. Hoffman achieved this record on a Thursday morning, May 3, 1975, in the amazing time of 22.3 minutes, so—God forbid—the house shouldn't be dirty when the cleaning woman came.

* * *

BEDMAKING

The fastest clocked time for bedmaking by a fastidious housewife was achieved by Debra Rachmil of Omaha, Nebraska. On the morning of May 6, 1977, a surprise phone call informed Mrs. Rachmil that out-of-town relatives would drop by for a visit in 10 minutes. Galvanized into action, she immediately made up two twin, one double, one queen-size, and one king-size bed in the unbelievable time of 32 seconds. The most remarkable fact about this feat was that two of the beds were occupied at the time by her son and husband, both of whom sustained minor abrasions and contusions as she punched them up while fluffing the pillows.

Heroism

TOP WOMAN ACE

The record for the greatest number of kills in aerial dogfights belong to Lt. Col. Naomi von Rothkowitz of the Israeli Air Force. During the 1967 Arab-Israeli War, in a single day of aerial combat over the Egyptian sector, Naomi brought down sixteen enemy planes. She shot down the first eight planes before she ran out of ammunition, and the other eight she nagged down.

*   *   *

MOST HEROIC RELATIVE

While attending a Seder on the first night of Passover in 1968, Max Lefkowitz, age 47, of Patterson, New Jersey, without regard to personal danger, saved his entire family from acute indigestion by throwing himself bodily across a ninth platter of gefilte fish, sustaining second-degree horseradish burns.

CHAPTER 12

Sports and Games

Track and Field

FASTEST MILE RELAY

The Yeshiva College mile relay team, competing in the 1969 Southern Baptist Invitational Games, shattered the world record for the mile relay by more than 11 seconds, only to be disqualified for using a 7-foot Hebrew National salami as a baton.

Football

MOST FUMBLES, SINGLE GAME

Promising rookie blocking-back, Sidney Pincus, of the Los Angeles Rams, was suddenly converted to running-back in the 1968 season opener, when the star was injured on the first play. Pincus carried the ball 35 times and fumbled it on every carry because he couldn't stand to touch the pigskin.

SHORTEST CAREER

See Sidney Picus, above.

*   *   *

LONGEST CAREER

Special team utility man Max "Man Mountain" Margolis has been on the Minnesota Viking roster for 34 years and is still going strong at the age of 53. The 6-foot, 10-inch, 732-pound Margolis has proved invaluable to the Viking squad, especially during the freezing winter home games. His huge *tochis* (behind), measuring 9 feet across, makes his services as designated Bench-Warmer in great demand by the entire team.

Swimming

SLOWEST CHANNEL SWIMMER, WOMAN

The 21-mile English Channel swim from Dover to Cape Gris Nez, France, has been done by many women in under 20 hours. However, it took Bella Brodsky, an Israeli Sabra, more than 102 hours to swim the same distance. The reason for this was that her entire body was protected from chill with a thick coat of chicken fat, and she kept slipping out of the water.

SLOWEST CANAL SWIMMER, MAN

The 400-foot-wide Suez Canal normally takes about three minutes to cross for an average swimmer; but Israeli soldier Dovid Ben Simon required 48 minutes to swim this short distance. This happened during the 1967 war, when Arab soldiers were shooting at him and he had to swim all the way underwater.

Baseball

SPORTS FUNERAL, BEST ATTENDED

Home-run king, Irving "Babe" Roth, superstar of the House of David baseball team whose overall lifetime batting average was .506, was unfortunately swept overboard while deep-sea fishing and lost at sea at the peak of his career. In his honor, a memorial service was held at the Yankee Stadium so that all his fans could pay their last respects. More than 80,000 people attended, and in the absence of their hero, "Babe" Roth, the pall-bearers carried in a coffin containing a Designated Corpse.

Jewish Olympic Games

ORIGINS

Biblical and archeological scholars agree that
the first so-called Jewish Olympic Games
(originally named the Mt. Sinai Games) took
place sometime during the Golden Age of the
Kings of Israel. The games began as religious
celebrations commemorating certain legendary

heroes of the Hebrew people. The earliest Jewish Olympic Games on record commemorated the heroic escape of the Israelites from Egypt and their pursuit by the Pharoah's soldiers. This event was called the "Cross-Country Slave Chase," and the slaves always won in a miraculous finish. The event was subsequently dropped from the games on the basis of protests that the "miracle" was a *fix!*

Subsequent Jewish Olympic Games (held every 200 years) introduced various events, each highlighting some proud and glorious period of Jewish history. One extremely popular event acclaimed the Biblical hero, Samson, as a symbol of the strength and power of ancient Israeli warriors. Indeed, the competition was modeled after some of the legendary exploits of Samson, which included killing 1000 Philistines with the jawbone of an ass and killing 3000 more by pulling down the pillars of the temple so the roof fell in. Dubbed "The Philistine-Killing Event," this popular competition was later withdrawn from the games on the grounds that the mortality rate among Philistine competitors was much too high.

Other events were added that paid tribute to Jewish courage against overwhelming odds. One example was the popular marksmanship contest commemorating the David and Goliath confrontation, called the "Sling-Shot Event." This event also had to be discontinued, when it became apparent that 10-foot-tall Goliath-type Philistine adversaries were becoming an endangered species.*

With the destruction of Solomon's Temple, the sacking of Jerusalem; the deportation of countless captive Jews into Babylonia, Assyria, Egypt, Greece, Rome, etc.; and with all of the tribes of Israel enslaved and dispersed far and wide, it seemed like a pretty good time to discontinue the Jewish Olympic Games for a while.

Two thousand years later, however, on May 7, 1887, the Jewish Olympic Games of the modern era were inaugurated in Galicia and have continued since that time.

Gold medals are awarded to the victors, symbolizing the courage of Jewish heroes whom modern athletes attempt to emulate. The beautifully embossed heraldic design on the medal depicts crossed herrings rampant on a field of boiled potatoes.

---

* The complete extinction of 10-foot-tall Philistines is proven in modern times by the fact that not a single Philistine plays professional basketball.

MOST MEDALS

Mark Lipschitz (U.S.), the swimmer who won 14 gold medals at the 1908 games, left the stadium immediately after the meet to have them appraised.

*   *   *

SPECIAL EVENTS, MODERN

KARATE BAGEL BREAKING

The greatest feat of karate bagel breaking by hand was achieved by Menasha Schwartzman of Yonkers, New York, who represented the Black-Belt Bagel-Breakers of Temple Emanuel. Schwartzman, in a single, powerful stroke, shattered a stack of three dozen stale water bagels. Schwartzman also holds the record for shattering the greatest number of bones in one hand.

LONG-DISTANCE NAGGING

The world record for long-distance, nonstop nagging on the telephone is 104 hours, established January 2–7, 1976, by Mrs. Rivka Laskey of Queens, New York. Mrs. Laskey, who telephoned her husband at a Holiday Inn in San Diego, California, was prevented from extending this record even further by a painful cramp in her tongue.

CROSS-COUNTRY *KVETCH* (COM-PLAINING)

Mrs. Sarah Lichtman, accompanied by husband, Marvin, in a cross-country auto tour from Boston to San Francisco (a 2,782-mile journey), maintained an incessant flow of round-the-clock *kvetching* (complaining) for the entire trip, which took nine days, ten hours, and six minutes (15.7 *kvetches* per mile). The trip ended tragically, however, when her distraught and exhausted husband stopped the car in the middle of the Golden Gate Bridge and jumped, followed by Sarah, who *kvetched* all the way down.

*   *   *

MARATHON *SHLEP* (DRAG)

Mrs. Selma Levine, a 33-year-old housewife of Dayton, Ohio, holds the world's marathon *shlepping* record of 23 hours and 37 minutes, established on July 9, 1969. During this time period, Mrs. Levine, a mother of five children, managed to *shlep* them all to the doctor, the orthodontist, ballet lessons, trumpet and piano lessons, yoga lessons, a Bar Mitzvah, a Cousins Club, a visit to both sets of grandparents, her husband's office, a shoe store, and a photographer's shop to have their pictures taken. Permitting herself no stops for resting, she *shlepped* 99.2 percent of the time. Due to a history of excessive and continuous *shlepping* by their mother, all five children today can easily be spotted by their unique appearance: their right (or *shlepping*) arms are all at least 7 inches longer than their left arms.

*   *   *

220-YARD BARGAIN-BASEMENT HURDLES

On September 3, 1966, Mrs. Rhoda Lippman of The Bronx, New York, who had drawn the inside lane at the Alexander's Department Store annual half-price bargain-basement sale, jumped off after two false starts and took the lead when the doors opened at 9 A.M. Accelerating rapidly, she hurdled three floorwalkers, two perfume counters, a mannequin, and a stock clerk, reaching the bargain counter in 2.8 minutes. In a frenzied finish, she snatched a wig, a blouse, a bra, a pair of pantyhose, a pair of wedgies, and a skirt off the body of a startled salesgirl.

NEW EVENTS

For the forthcoming Jewish Olympics, which will be held in the Borscht Bowl, Catskill Mountains, New York, a new event—the Pentathlon—has been added. The five events include:

- Mt. Sinai Hill Climb
- Giant Downhill Shalom
- Free-Style Whiplash Dash
- Potato-Latke Throw (no applesauce)
- Heavyweight Burden of Guilt-Lifting

Here are 9 wacky, zany, all-in-good-fun, two-in-one joke books from ace comedian, Larry Wilde

Order the ones you want today!

Another tumultuous romantic novel
by Patricia Matthews,
author of the multi-million
copy national bestseller,
LOVE'S AVENGING HEART

Love's Wildest Promise

P40-047 $1.95

Sarah Moody was a lady's maid in a wealthy London home. But suddenly her quiet sheltered world was turned upside down when she was abducted and smuggled aboard a ship bound for the colonies. Its cargo—whores to satisfy the appetites of King George's soldiers in New York. Was Sarah destined to become one of these women? Or would she find the man she was searching for, the man who would help her to fulfill Love's Wildest Promise.

The epic novel of the Old South,
ablaze with the unbridled passions
of men and women seeking
new heights for their love

Windhaven Plantation

Marie de Jourlet

P40-022 $1.95

Here is the proud and passionate story of one man—
Lucien Bouchard. The second son of a French nobleman,
a man of vision and of courage, Lucien dares to seek a new
way of life in the New World that suits his own high
ideals. Yet his true romantic nature is at war with his
lusty, carnal desires. The four women in his life reflect
this raging conflict: Edmée, the high-born, amoral
French sophisticate who scorns his love, choosing his
elder brother, heir to the family title; Dimarte, the in-
genuous, earthy, and sensual Indian princess; Amelia,
the fiery free-spoken beauty who is trapped in a life of
servitude for crimes she didn't commit; and Priscilla,
whose proper manner hid the unbridled passion of her
true desires.

"... will satisfy avid fans of the plantation genre."
—*Bestsellers* magazine

If you can't find this book at your local bookstore, simply
send the cover price plus 25¢ for postage and handling to:

 Pinnacle Books
275 Madison Avenue, New York, New York 10016

THE MANITOU

"Like some mind-gripping drug, it has the uncanny ability to seize you and hold you firmly in its clutches from the moment you begin until you drop the book from your trembling fingers after you have finally finished the last page."
—Bernhardt J. Hurwood

Misquamacus—An American Indian sorcerer. In the seventeenth century he had sworn to wreak a violent vengeance upon the callous, conquering White Man. This was just before he died, over four hundred years ago. Now he has found an abominable way to return, the perfect birth for his revenge.

Karen Tandy—A slim, delicate, auburn-haired girl with an impish face. She has a troublesome tumor on the back of her neck, a tumor that no doctor in New York City can explain. It seems to be moving, growing, developing—almost as if it were alive! She is the victim of

THE MANITOU
GRAHAM MASTERTON

A Pinnacle Book
P982 $1.75

If you can't find this book at your local bookstore, simply send the cover price, plus 25¢ for postage and handling to:

PINNACLE BOOKS
275 Madison Avenue
New York, New York 10016